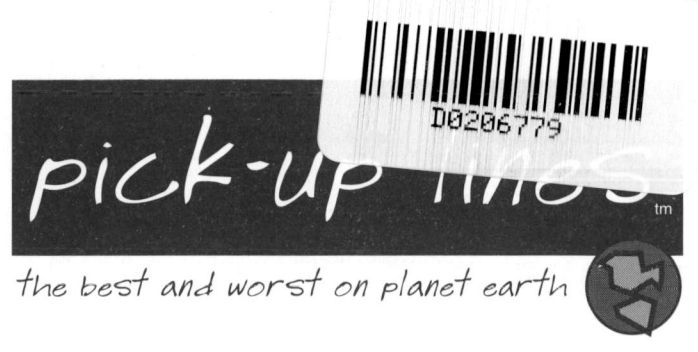

pick-up lines™

the best and worst on planet earth

a buzz boxx book

JOHN GRAHAM / STUART OUGH / MORGAN TAYLOR

Andrews and McMeel
A Universal Press Syndicate Company
Kansas City

 For information, write Andrews and McMeel, a Universal Press Syndicate Company, 4520 Main Street, Kansas City, Missouri 64111.

ISBN 0-8362-2198-2

Library of Congress Catalog Card Number: 96-84514

buzz boxx

Who are we?

the lost generation . . . slackers . . . generation x . . . whiners . . . whatever. welcome to buzz boxx.

buzz boxx is a product company of, for, and about young people. buzz boxx is made up of talented young people from various backgrounds who create, make, and sell products intended for our peers. sorry, no big 50-year-old v.p. of marketing trying to dictate what we should like and buy. after all, we know what we like best. it's a means for us to express ourselves in a positive way and bring some smiles to people's faces. remember, life is way too short. make a positive difference by what you do in the world around.

we're buzz boxx - the voice of young america

The buzz boxx team for this book includes:

John Graham—company mastermind
Stuart Ough—copy kat
Morgan Taylor—creative commissioner

Thanks to our families, friends, and friends of friends who shared their favorite pick-up lines with us.

INTRO

So, is that a book in your pocket or are you just happy to see me? Haven't you ever wondered where some people get their lines? So did we, and you won't believe some of the lines people have used or had used on them! Now all of our "scientifically conducted research," gathered from friends, strangers, and those popular havens for pick-up artists, is found right here in this book. *Pick-Up Lines: The Best and Worst on Planet Earth,* includes everything from the classics, to the creative, to the downright bold. Of course, we don't guarantee that every line is for everybody, but we do bet many will bring a smile. So, flip through the pages, learn a few, and next time you're admiring someone from afar and feel the urge, walk up and see what happens.

Want a date? Get this book!

GENERAL
ADVISORY
FUNNY LINES

Warning. This book is not intended for all audiences. It is in no way, shape, or form intended to be a self-help manual or to be taken too seriously. The surgeon general's secretary warns against the use of this book if you're easily offended, inherited a weak bladder, or happen to be a pregnant woman wearing a large floral pattern and those fuzzy slippers—you have enough to worry about. Otherwise it is rather safe—go ahead and read the whole thing. **buzz boxx** takes no responsibility for injuries as the result of uncontrolled laughter or as a result of actually trying some of these lines. So, we really take no responsibility for much of anything. Enjoy, and remember, play safe.

P.S. If you've read all of this and you're still offended by the book, get a life; you're taking it way too seriously.

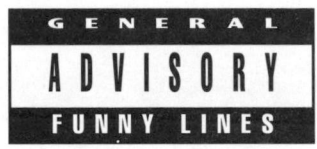

pick-up lines™

the best and worst on planet earth

Hi, can we pretend that I used some line that worked really well and move on to the next stage?

STUART O.
INDIANAPOLIS, IN

(ASK FOR A QUARTER)

I'LL FLIP YOU. HEADS-YOUR PLACE. TAILS-MY PLACE.

ANONYMOUS

Mmm, mmm-I'd like to get me some of that!

DAVIS R.
NASHVILLE, TN

Do you kiss with your eyes open or shut?

CONNA G.
PEACHTREE CITY, GA

Are you related to Adonis?

LEIGH F.
ANN ARBOR, MI

You travel a lot, don't you? I've seen you many times at the Atlanta airport.

(AT AN AIRPORT)

ELIZABETH D.
CINCINNATI, OH

IF GOOD LOOKS WERE AGAINST THE LAW YOU'D BE ARRESTED, BOOKED, AND JAILED FOR A LIFE.

BRYCE M.
ST. LOUIS, MO

I've got an alarm clock that makes the best sounds in the morning. Would you like to come over and hear it?

SEAN P.
INDIANAPOLIS, IN

You're all that and then some!

CEDRIC W.
TEANECK, NJ

Do you believe in angels? Because I think I'm looking at one.

TODD R.
PORTLAND, OR

HI, MY NAME IS ANITA . . . ANITA MAN.

CHASS K.
INDIANAPOLIS, IN

How are you guys doing tonight? (ARM AROUND HER)

ANONYMOUS

I'm an army recruiter. Why don't you come over to my place and "be all you can be."

YUSEF A.
INDIANAPOLIS, IN

I must have died and gone to heaven 'cause you're the most beautiful angel I've ever seen!

ELENA K.
KENOSHA, WI

You realize since I'm in the army I can do more in one hour than most men can do all night!

YUSEF A.
INDIANAPOLIS, IN

I bet you were voted "most attractive" in high school.

MITCHELL L.
ROSWELL, GA

Can I have your autograph? I'm your biggest fan.

KIM D.
MUNCIE, IN

OH BABY, WHAT'S UP? OH, YOU LOOK SO FINE, LOOK AT YOU.

CURTIS J.
ST. LOUIS, MO

I'm really into dangerous guys. So, out on bail?

JESSICA R.
BLOOMINGTON, IN

Is that a banana in your pocket or are you just happy to see me?

ANONYMOUS

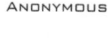

My birth control prescription runs out tomorrow. Should I refill?

CINDY K.
INDIANAPOLIS, IN

Pardon me, bartender. What do you have that's cool, smooth, and tasty?

BRENT B.
CINCINNATI, OH

You're like a prize-winning bass. I don't know whether to mount you or eat you!

MATT B.
INDIANAPOLIS, IN

Nice belt—but I think it would look better wrapped around my neck.

TERRI R.
BOCA RATON, FL

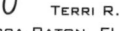

My friends bet me I couldn't get you to kiss me.

BILL W.
ZIONSVILLE, IN

I BET you look GOOD IN A BIKINI.

JULIE K.
LA CROSSE, WI

I have a $100 bill hidden on my body. Care to find out? One hint, it's not in my pockets.

MATT I.
MUNCIE, IN

You da bomb!

Keith H.
Milwaukee, WI

YOU'RE SUCH A VISION OF BEAUTY, I BET EVEN BLIND MEN SWEAR THEY CAN SEE YOU.

CARLOS D.
TUCSON, AZ

Are you a natural blonde? I guess there's only one way to tell.

ANONYMOUS

I'd like to blow your mind—as well as a few other things.

ANONYMOUS

I'm tired of people respecting me for my brain and not my body. Can you help me?

JEREMY F.
CHAMPAIGN, IL

Aren't you a body double in the movies?

DAN U.
COLUMBIA, SC

The book you're reading, I hear it's wonderful!

(AT A BOOKSTORE)

JASMINE K.
BERKELEY, CA

How do you like your eggs: fried, scrambled, or poached?

ANONYMOUS

NICE BOOTS—WANT TO KNOCK 'EM?

NAOMI D.
SYRACUSE, NY

Do you know the way you drink from a bottle is how you kiss?

MARY F.
MEMPHIS, TN

Boxers or briefs?

SUSAN W.
KNOXVILLE, TN

I see you and think, God must be making up for lost time after sending me to an all-boys school.

BRADLEY B.
GREENWICH, CT

Can I buy you breakfast in the morning?

ANONYMOUS

I like my EGGS OVER EASy.

TIM B.
INDIANAPOLIS, IN

Hello? Oh, your body was calling me from across the room.

Reggie K.
Peoria, IL

Are you a friend of the bride or groom?

(AT A WEDDING)

KELLI W.
BOSTON, MA

Excuse me, but are those Bugle Boy jeans that you're wearing?

GINA D.
COLUMBIA, MD

(BUMP INTO THEM) Oops.

KRISTINA K.
MILWAUKEE, WI

I bet your dad's a baker, 'cause baby, you got some great buns.

DAVID B.
SHAKER HEIGHTS, OH

Excuse me, waiter, are my buns hot?

BECKY F.
COLORADO SPRINGS, CO

Nice butt (but) . . . I think it's going to rain tomorrow.

(PAUSE MIDSENTENCE AND DETERMINE IF YOU NEED THE SAVE)

PERRY M.
FT. LAUDERDALE, FL

I think I should be committed to an insane asylum 'cause you drive me crazy.

BILL M.
CLEARWATER, FL

It looks like we're going in the same direction. Want to share a cab?

JACKIE T.
CHICAGO, IL

(GIVE THEM A QUARTER AND YOUR PHONE NUMBER)
Call me sometime.

LYDIA V.
ST. LOUIS, MO

Do you like candy bars? Because I've got a Milky Way for you.

ANONYMOUS

Do you like candy bars? Because I've got a Butterfinger that will make you Snicker and scream Oh, Henry!

ANONYMOUS

Care for a Certs? You might just need it by the end of the night.

LOUIS R.
AUSTIN, TX

HI, MY NAME IS CHANCE. DO I HAVE ONE?

CHANCE H.
INDIANAPOLIS, IN

Do you think I'm cute or haven't you had enough to drink yet?

MELISSA S.
BATON ROUGE, LA

I bet you look really good in chaps . . . and nothing else.

JENNILEE B.
DALLAS, TX

You must be a chef, because you certainly are mighty spicy.

GLEN O.
BROOKFIELD, WI

I like a talented woman. So, can you tie a knot in a cherry stem with your tongue?

KRISTIN C.
BLOOMINGTON, IN

Nice chest—how many days a week do you work out?

ELIZABETH D.
CINCINNATI, OH

I BET WE'D MAKE BEAUTIFUL CHILDREN TOGETHER.

RHONDA C.
FT. WAYNE, IN

I bet you'd be more comfortable without any clothes on.

JOHN B.
BLOOMINGTON, IN

Do you know CPR? I hope so because you're so beautiful I'm having a heart attack.

RUSSELL S.
EDINA, MN

I know you. Didn't you go to (YOUR COLLEGE NAME HERE)?

HEATHER W.
MEMPHIS, TN

YOU SMELL REALLY GOOD. WHAT COLOGNE ARE YOU WEARING?

JON G.
EAU CLAIRE, WI

Do you come here often?

ANONYMOUS

I just wanted to come over and introduce myself, because I have the feeling that I'll see you again.

MIKE D.
CHICAGO, IL

Would you like to go back to my place and be two consenting adults?

EDDIE R.
EVANSTON, IL

Do you wear colored contacts or are your eyes so naturally beautiful?

CHANTAL P.
NASHVILLE, TN

Are you in the mood for dessert?

Mike G.
Indianapolis, IN

You remind me of a crescent wrench . . .
every time I see you my nuts tighten up.

JEFF C.
CEDAR RAPIDS, IA

Do you think I'm cute?

ANONYMOUS

(STARE 'EM DOWN. BITE LOWER LIP.) **DAMN!**

MIKE G.
INDIANAPOLIS, IN

Would you like to dance?

ANONYMOUS

I can tell you're a man who's a little dangerous.

CYNDY P.
SAN MATEO, CA

Excuse me, I'm _____. What's your name, because in my dream last night I only called you "Darling."

MOLLY H.
TACOMA, WA

Do you believe in fairy tales, because I bet we could live happily ever after.

KEVIN N.
PORTSMOUTH, VA

What do you know about dates?

(AT A GROCERY STORE)

ALICIA N.
PLANO, TX

I hope our daughter looks just like you.

JEANETTE C.
ATHENS, GA

Miss December, right?

CHARLENE T.
AUSTIN, TX

What's a beautiful girl like you doing decorating a wall?

SHAWNESSY O.
TERRE HAUTE, IN

Wow! I think I just had a déjà vu because the last time you agreed to have dinner with me.

SHELBY C.
PHILADELPHIA, PA

Hi, my name is Dick . . . Dick Fitzwell.

MORGAN T.
INDIANAPOLIS, IN

You're amazing! You make the women I dream about look short, fat, and balding.

KURT K.
SCOTTSDALE, AZ

I was looking in the dictionary, and there isn't a word that fully describes your beauty.

WILLIAM S.
PHILADELPHIA, PA

Will you have dinner with me tonight?

ANONYMOUS

When are you buying me dinner?

TIM B.
INDIANAPOLIS, IN

With each second that passes, we're getting closer to death. Live a little and have a drink with me.

TREY J.
PALO ALTO, CA

Excuse me, can you tell me the best way to meet someone like you?

STACEY B.
EVANSTON, IL

Hi. I'm going to be a doctor.

CHARLES V.
ATLANTA, GA

Do you believe in love at first sight, or do I have to walk by you again?

WES R.
LAKEWOOD, CO

Excuse me doctor, but in your professional opinion, how do I look?

PAULA H.
PITTSBURGH, PA

Pinch me. I must be dreaming.

DENNIS M.
WILMETTE, IL

Nice dress—I bet it would look really good at the foot of my bed.

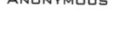

ANONYMOUS

LIFE ISN'T A DRESS REHEARSAL, SO I JUST HAD TO FIND OUT IF YOU'RE THE ONE.

PETER H.
CHICAGO, IL

Can I buy you a drink?

ANONYMOUS

What are you drinking?

ANONYMOUS

BEFORE YOU RUN, I AM NOT A FREAK.

COLLEENE M.
INDIANAPOLIS, IN

Can I buy you a drink . . . in Tahiti?

TERESA H.
EVANSTON, IL

Can I buy you a drink? How about a "Screaming Orgasm"?

DONNIE H.
SOUTH BEND, IN

If there is any truth to "drop-dead gorgeous" then I'm stone cold and 6 feet under right now.

STEVE S.
GREENFIELD, WI

Isn't this elevator really slow?

STACY G.
NEW YORK, NY

YOUR BLUE EYES ARE THE COLOR OF A CLEAR BLUE SEA, AND I COULD SWIM IN THEM FOREVER.

MARK S.
CHAMPAIGN, IL

You know, you can tell a person's thoughts by the look in their eyes, and I like what you're thinking.

SCOTT P.
SAN MATEO, CA

If your brain has as many curves as your body, you've got to be Einstein!

MARJORIE N.
OXFORD, OH

You know, you can tell a person's thoughts by the look in their eyes. Can you tell what I'm thinking?

SCOTT P.
SAN MATEO, CA

Hi, I'm famous. My line is in a book.

XEN C.
INDIANAPOLIS, IN

ARE YOU FAMOUS? I BET YOU'RE A MODEL.

ANONYMOUS

Yeah, a night with me isn't like fast food-
it's a seven-course meal.

DALE T.
KNOXVILLE, TN

Ooooh, you got that look . . . the look that says,
"I want a fat woman."

DARRYL P.
MILWAUKEE, WI

Do you believe in fate?

ANONYMOUS

Beauty like yours is like a ghost, many have heard about it but few have actually seen it.

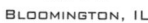

Hope T.
Bloomington, IL

Will you be the father of my children?

TAMMY H.
INDIANAPOLIS, IN

Do you believe in love at first sight?

ANONYMOUS

Would you like to go back to my room and see my fish tank?

CYNTHIA M.
LOS ANGELES, CA

Excuse me, your fly is down. Oops, maybe not now, but definitely later.

JULIE N.
MINNEAPOLIS, MN

I'm a sensitive '90s kind of guy. I believe in a lot of foreplay. How about you?

ANONYMOUS

i'm free tomorrow night.

ANONYMOUS

Excuse me, I don't mean to embarrass you, but you are absolutely stunning.

ERIC D,
NASHVILLE, TN

Don't you just love the french fries here?

LISETTE R.
FT. WORTH, TX

Stuart? Oh, I'm sorry, you look just like a good friend of mine.

MELISSA C.
BLOOMINGTON, IN

HI, I AM NOT A FROG.

STEPHEN R.
ANN ARBOR, MI

You . . . Me . . . F###!

Tyler S.
Chicago, IL

Excuse me, do you f### or do I owe you an apology?

Anonymous

Let's Go.

Rick H.
Kansas City, MO

Do you know that a smile uses fewer muscles than a frown? And baby, I'd really like to put a grin on your face.

THOMAS W.
BALTIMORE, MD

God must have created you on a Saturday so he could take Sunday off to admire his work.

Christina B.
Grosse Pointe, MI

Damn, baby, I bet God celebrated after making you.

Marvin H.
Tampa, FL

When God made you, I bet he broke the mold.

Carrie R.
Pittsburgh, PA

Damn! No wonder God rested on the seventh day.

CARRIE R.
PITTSBURGH, PA

Love goddess in another life, right?

PERRY M.
FT. LAUDERDALE, FL

GIRL, YOU GOT IT GOING ON!

CEDRIC W.
TEANECK, NJ

Is it hot in here or is it just you?

KIM B.
LAFAYETTE, IN

I want to kiss you the way Clark Gable kissed Vivien Leigh in Gone with the Wind.

JANINE B.
SAN FRANCISCO, CA

Your body is like a gospel–I could sing praises to it all day.

JASON O.
CLEVELAND, OH

Haven't I seen you on the cover of GQ?

KELLEY L.
DAYTON, OH

Guess what? If you buy two of those, the third one is free.

(AT A GROCERY STORE)

CHRISTINE J.
WEST PEORIA, IL

You've got great hair. Can I run my fingers through it?

ADRIA G.
CHICAGO, IL

GREAT HAIR—I'D LIKE TO SEE IF IT LOOKS AS GOOD IN THE MORNING.

WENDY P.
ST. PETERSBURG, FL

You look like my first husband . . .
and I've never been married.

JULIE S.
INDIANAPOLIS, IN

You know what they say about guys with big hands . . .

ANONYMOUS

I can tell by the way you move your hands that you're very limber.

ELIZABETH D.
CINCINNATI, OH

I've been told I'm really good with my hands.

ANONYMOUS

Tall . . . dark . . . hi handsome!

JENNA M.
CHICAGO, IL

Do you want to play my harp or would you like to pluck my strings?

ELIZABETH O. (A HARPIST)
CARMEL, IN

Haven't I seen you at the health club?

ANONYMOUS

(LEAN IN AND LOOK CLOSE)

Yep, I'm positive . . . your lips were made for kissing.

VICKI E.
MADISON, WI

Can you call 911 for me? I think my heart stopped beating when I saw you.

GAYLE C.
RALEIGH, NC

YOU SURE LOOK GOOD. HOW WAS HEAVEN WHEN YOU LEFT IT?

MATTHEW T.
PITTSBURGH, PA

Didn't it hurt when you fell from the heavens?

ANONYMOUS

Hi.

STUART O.
INDIANAPOLIS, IN

Didn't we go to different high schools together?

GWENNE C.
CHARLESTON, SC

(WITH A TOTAL STRANGER) Wow! It's been so long since I've seen you. Are you going to our high school reunion?

IAN D.
SEATTLE, WA

YOUR BODY IS LIKE A GOSPEL,
AND I'M SHOUTING
"LORDY, LORDY!"

LIONEL C.
PHILADELPHIA, PA

Dag, with hips like that I think we ought to get the swerve on.

KEVIN M.
NEW YORK, NY

You know, I can hog-tie a calf in under 6 seconds.

BRANDON E.
TULSA, OK

IF I TOLD YOU THAT YOU HAD A HOT BODY, WOULD YOU HOLD IT AGAINST ME?

MELANIE H.
LOS ANGELES, CA

I'm GOING to HAWAII ON VACATION NEXT MONTH. HOW ABOUT JOINING ME AND MAKING IT A HONEYMOON?

CINDY K.
INDIANAPOLIS, IN

Care to dance? How about the horizontal bop?

ANONYMOUS

Is it hot in here or what?

ANONYMOUS

I bet "gorgeous" is your middle name.

ANONYMOUS

Can I buy you a house someday?

CATHY K.
HOBOKEN, NJ

You're so beautiful it hurts to look at you.

AMIE F.
SALT LAKE CITY, UT

I've never wanted to be an ice-cream cone so bad in all my life.

BEN J.
PORTLAND, OR

Girl, the things I want to do with you are illegal in 27 states.

ANONYMOUS

WHAT'S THE BEST WAY TO MAKE A GOOD FIRST IMPRESSION WITH YOU?

STACEY B.
EVANSTON, IL

They say you have only one chance to make a first impression. How am I doing so far?

KIM L.
INDIANAPOLIS, IN

You must drink milk, because,
damn, it sure does your body good.

April W.
Noblesville, IN

I'm a math teacher. Can I show you infinity?

HUNTER V.
PASADENA, CA

You're like a finely crafted instrument. May I play with you?

GAVIN F.
BOSTON, MA

Do you have any Irish in you? Would you like to?

MORGAN T.
INDIANAPOLIS, IN

God, I'd love to be your pair of jeans.

MARK W.
OMAHA, NE

DO YOU KISS ON THE FIRST DATE?

ANONYMOUS

(HAND SOMEONE A $1 BILL) I bet I can kiss you on the lips without touching you. (KISS THEM) Oops, I guess I lost.

SUSAN A.
CEDAR RAPIDS, IA

I really like a woman with
straight hair. Huh, a pity . . .
one night with me and it's sure
to curl with pleasure.

TIM L.
TEMPE, AZ

HERE I AM. USE ME, ABUSE ME, TOSS ME AWAY LIKE AN OLD KLEENEX.

GREGORY G.
SYRACUSE, NY

Do you mind if I sit down? When I saw you I went weak in the knees.

COURTNEY C.
ST. PAUL, MN

You look like someone I should know.

NATHAN B.
FREMONT, CA

You look like someone I know.

ANONYMOUS

Don't I know you?

DARCIE W.
ATLANTA, GA

CAN I DO YOUR LAUNDRY? I'VE ALWAYS DREAMED OF GETTING IN THE PANTS OF A WOMAN LIKE YOU.

LANCE F.
MILWAUKEE, WI

Oh my! There is a God!

Dawn D.
New York, NY

Are you legal?

JEFF R.
ZIONSVILLE, IN

Can you help me? I'm a lesbian trapped in a man's body.

ANONYMOUS

Excuse me, but do you have a license to carry those in public?

JAMES G.
ATHENS, GA

You're so sweet that one lick and I bet my teeth would fall out. Care to find out?

ANONYMOUS

Life is too short. Go home with me tonight.

ANONYMOUS

I'm free the rest of my life.

JAMIE F.
ANDERSON, IN

Hercules has nothing on you.

Brenda S.
Germantown, TN

Do you have a light?

ANONYMOUS

My name is ____. How do you like me so far?

CASEY S.
INDIANAPOLIS, IN

Your lips were made to be kissed, and I hate to see a good thing go to waste.

VICKI E.
MADISON, WI

As soon as I saw your face, I realized I'd only then started living.

LAURIE R.
INDIANAPOLIS, IN

Ah baby, you sure look good tonight.

REMI A.
INDIANAPOLIS, IN

Haven't I seen you before? Maybe in a magazine somewhere?

NEAL G.
INDIANAPOLIS, IN

Nice ass!

ANONYMOUS

Who says male chivalry is dead. Care to join me for an orgasm?

MORGAN T.
INDIANAPOLIS, IN

Are you married?

ANONYMOUS

Girl, if you were a McDonald's Extra Value Meal, I'd definitely like to super-size you.

HAROLD W.
INDIANAPOLIS, IN

I'M LOOKING FOR A GIFT FOR MY BROTHER, AND YOU LOOK LIKE THE SAME SIZE. CAN I MEASURE THIS ON YOU?

(BROTHER NOT NECESSARY)

JENEE W.
LAFAYETTE, IN

NICE MELONS.

(AT A GROCERY STORE)

JERRY B.
SOUTH BEND, IN

I'm speaking for all men when I say this: Men look at you and they see a beautiful woman.

ELIZABETH D.
CINCINNATI, OH

Mmm, mmm. With a body like that I'm surprised your father lets you out of the house.

Donald I.
Peoria, IL

Haven't we met somewhere before?

ANONYMOUS

You must be tired, 'cause you've been runnin' through my mind all day.

ANONYMOUS

I DON'T WANT TO F### WITH YOUR MIND, JUST YOUR BODY.

ANONYMOUS

YOU'RE THE KIND OF GIRL WHO'D MAKE ME CONSIDER A MINIVAN.

LORI A.
INDIANAPOLIS, IN

I've got only two words for you: Mmm! Mmm!

DARREN H.
ORLANDO, FL

You're related to Jennifer Aniston, aren't you?

KATEY P.
SAN DIEGO, CA

Ouch!

BRENT L.
INDIANAPOLIS, IN

How much money do you make?

TABATHA D.
INDIANAPOLIS, IN

Can I borrow a quarter? I promised I'd call my mother when I found the woman I'm going to marry.

JED M.
GREENWOOD, IN

Don't our mothers play bridge together?

TROY S.
BLOOMFIELD HILLS, MI

Didn't our mothers go to the same high school together?

TROY S.
BLOOMFIELD HILLS, MI

What's your name?

ANONYMOUS

Hi, my name is ______. Do we know each other well enough now for me to ask you out?

AARON J.
COLUMBUS, OH

Hi, you just got a phone call. It was your mom and she said it was okay if you come home with me tonight.

PETER S.
EVANSVILLE, IN

I bet you have a beautiful name to go with a face like yours.

CHAD N.
IOWA CITY, IA

OUR NAMES WOULD LOOK GREAT ON NAPKINS TOGETHER.

ALLISON M.
RICHMOND, VA

Would you mind if I looked at your newspaper when you're finished?

(ON THE BUS)

MARY ANNE F.
CHICAGO, IL

I noticed you from across the way.

ANONYMOUS

Do you know what would look really good on you? Me!

GEORGE O.
DENVER, CO

Hi, have you ever wanted to have a one-night sland?

ANONYMOUS

YOU MUST BE ONE OF "AMERICA'S MOST WANTED" WITH A KILLER BODY LIKE THAT.

JUAN C.
DALLAS, TX

Great pants–they'd look better on my floor.

JAMES T.
SKOKIE, IL

HI, MY PARENTS ARE GONE FOR THE NIGHT.

JEFF R.
ZIONSVILLE, IN

Do you believe in reincarnation, because I could swear that we were lovers in a past life.

LAWRENCE F.
DES MOINES, IA

(HOLD OUT A PENNY) A penny for my thoughts or fifty bucks to act them out.

ANONYMOUS

Is that a Wonderbra, or are your breasts naturally perky?

BETH Y.
CHICAGO, IL

I HAVE TO KNOW, IS IT MY GOOD LOOKS OR CHARMING PERSONALITY THAT YOU'RE ATTRACTED TO?

ANDY H.
SOUTH BEND, IN

Shhh . . . can you hear that?
It's my heart pounding
for you.

CHARLES A.
LOS ANGELES, CA

I've lost my phone number,
can I borrow yours?

MARINA R.
WEST LAFAYETTE, IN

What do you think the artist was thinking with that painting?

(AT A GALLERY)

JENNY Q.
SAN FRANCISCO, CA

HOW ABOUT A PIZZA AND A F###? . . .
OR MAYBE YOU DON'T LIKE PIZZA.

SEAN G.
EVANSVILLE, IN

What's an amazing person like you doing in a place like this?

Rick V.
Madison, WI

Didn't I see you in *Playboy*?

Katey P.
San Diego, CA

What do you say we blow this pop stand?

Anonymous

Do you believe in a fairy godmother, 'cause I think I'm looking at my handsome prince.

JASON V.
MOBILE, AL

Do you believe in God? 'Cause you're the answer to my prayers.

LISA Z.
LANSING, MI

Excuse me, but are you wearing f.m. pumps?

ANONYMOUS

What a cute puppy! How old is he?

(ANYWHERE WITH A PUPPY)

SUSAN S.
SAN DIEGO, CA

CAN I BORROW YOUR RAY-BANS? YOUR SMILE REALLY LIGHTS UP THIS ROOM.

PAMELA H.
DALLAS, TX

ARE THOSE REAL?

TIM B.
INDIANAPOLIS, IN

Would you like to go back to my place and check out my record collection?

JENNIFER C.
NASHVILLE, TN

Can I borrow a quarter? I promised I'd call my mother when I fell in love.

JED M.
GREENWOOD, IN

I see a long-term relationship forming with you. I'm in love with you.

ELIZABETH D.
CINCINNATI, OH

Trust me, I'll respect you for your brain as well as your body.

MITCHELL L.
ROSWELL, GA

I hope you know how to do mouth-to-mouth resuscitation, 'cause you really take my breath away.

CHAD N.
IOWA CITY, IA

What size ring do you wear?

ANONYMOUS

GIRL, I WANT TO ROCK YOUR WORLD.

ALTON M.
CLEVELAND, OH

Baby, my love rocket will take you beyond the stars.

ANONYMOUS

Screw me if I'm wrong, but is your name Yasmanina?

(OR ANY OTHER OBSCURE NAME)

CHRIS T.
BLOOMINGTON, IN

Baby, you must like to sail, because the way you walk really raises my anchor.

RICHARD A.
CLEVELAND, OH

The last time I saw something as heavenly the clouds parted and the cherubs sang.

LIONEL C.
PHILADELPHIA, PA

I JUST HAD NEW SHOCKS PUT ON MY CAR. CARE TO HELP ME TEST THEM?

GREGG D.
COLUMBUS, OH

Nice shoes—they'd look great under my bed tomorrow.

ANONYMOUS

You're the first man that I've seen all day who really takes care of his shoes.

MICHELLE E.
SAN ANTONIO, TX

Your body's like a shrine that I could worship all day long.

MERIT H.
BOSTON, MA

Hi, I'm MR. Right. SOMEONE said you WERE looking for me.

STEWART H.
LEXINGTON, KY

I'm really kind of shy, but I saw you and knew I had to get over myself and meet you.

PAUL W.
SOUTHFIELD, MI

I'm usually not very good with lines so I won't even try.

MATT O.
CEDAR RAPIDS, IA

What's your sign?

ANONYMOUS

BABY, WHEN THEY MADE DANGEROUS CURVES AHEAD SIGNS THEY MUST HAVE BEEN TALKIN' ABOUT YOU.

BARRY M.
DES MOINES, IA

Excuse me, but where are your glass slippers?

RUBIN F.
MINNEAPOLIS, MN

You smell great. Can I eat you?

ANONYMOUS

What's your sign?
Let me guess-
Caution: Dangerous Curves.

Barry M.
Des Moines, IA

Great smile—I bet your dentist is very proud of you.

Holly S.
Evanston, IL

Do you smoke? Good, neither do I.

Cindy K.
Indianapolis, IN

I'm under your spell.

Quentin H.
Cambridge, MA

Would you mind spotting me on this machine?

(AT A HEALTH CLUB)

SHERRI A.
BALTIMORE, MD

I couldn't help but notice <u>me</u> staring at <u>you</u>.

BOYD R.
NEW ORLEANS, LA

I couldn't help but notice <u>you</u> staring at <u>me</u>.

BOYD R.
NEW ORLEANS, LA

CAN YOU DO A FAVOR FOR ME? NEXT TIME YOU SEE YOUR PARENTS, BE SURE TO THANK THEM FOR ME.

SCOTT C.
NEW YORK, NY

WEREN'T YOU IN THE SPORTS ILLUSTRATED SWIMSUIT ISSUE?

KATEY P.
SAN DIEGO, CA

Do you prefer Lean Cuisine or Stouffers?

(AT A GROCERY STORE)

VICKI E.
INDIANAPOLIS, IN

(PREMEDITATED MOVE, BUT HAVE AND DROP STRING FROM HAND)

LOOK! I COME WITH NO STRINGS ATTACHED.

ROB H.
FISHERS, IN

Give me some sugar, baby.

JANICE M.
JEFFERSONVILLE, IN

I'd like to see the sun rise in your eyes.

TERI C.
SACRAMENTO, CA

I finally met a girl I could take home to mom.
So what are you doing Sunday?

LAURIE A.
INDIANAPOLIS, IN

Boy, that smile sure looks good on you.

JULIE K.
MADISON, WI

I bet you taste really good.

ANONYMOUS

NICE TATTOOS—DO YOU HAVE ANY MORE THAT I CAN'T SEE?

CHRIS H.
BLOOMINGTON, IN

I love your tie. Did you buy it here?

(AT A CLOTHING STORE)

CATHERINE L.
RICHARDSON, TX

Do you HAVE THE TIME?

ANONYMOUS

Want to see my sex organ? (STICK OUT YOUR TONGUE)

DAN E.
INDIANAPOLIS, IN

I was trying to say something smooth, but your beauty makes me tongue-tied.

ELIZABETH S.
BOWLING GREEN, KY

Your father must be the world's greatest thief, because he stole the stars and put them in your eyes.

SHANNON M.
INDIANAPOLIS, IN

You're so sweet that I bet one kiss would give me a toothache.

COREY K.
DENVER, CO

A question has been bothering me for some time. How many licks does it take to get to the center of your Tootsie Pop?

ANONYMOUS

(TAP YOUR FINGER ON HIS SHOULDER AND BEGIN TO COUNT OUT LOUD)

How many times do I have to touch you before you ask me out?

CLARISSA D.
CARBONDALE, IL

Are my eyes playing tricks on me or are you really this gorgeous?!

TAYLOR H.
GREEN BAY, WI

YOU REMIND ME OF A BUTTERBALL TURKEY—I WANT TO STUFF YOU, BASTE YOU, AND HEAT YOU UP UNTIL YOUR BUTTON POPS.

MELODY J.
PRINCETON, NJ

You're so good looking I bet your mother's still turning heads.

DARREL B.
ARLINGTON, VA

For you, I'D SHARE my toothBRUSH.

MARSHA D.
LOS ANGELES, CA

The twinkle in your eyes puts the stars to shame.

AMY N.
ST. LOUIS PARK, MN

When they created the alphabet, they should have put "U" and "I" together.

BRENDA S.
DAYTON, OH

(LOOK ALL OVER HIS BODY, LIFT UP HIS ARMS, ETC.)

Don't mind me, I'm just looking for your USDA prime grade beef stamp.

JACI P.
DES MOINES, IA

Voulez-vous coucher avec moi ce soir?

(IT'S FRENCH, LOOK IT UP)

ANONYMOUS

Excuse me, waitress, but your buns are hot!

TERRENCE C.
ST. LOUIS, MO

Hi, I'm the kind of guy your mother warned you about. (FLASH BIG SMILE)

STEWART H.
LEXINGTON, KY

You've mamboed . . . you've tangoed . . . you've twisted . . . but have you ever really danced between the sheets?!

ANONYMOUS

I BET YOU HAVE A WASHBOARD STOMACH.

CYNTHIA M.
LOS ANGELES, CA

I have a water bed. Want to make some waves?

ALAN N.
AMHERST, NY

Pardon me, do you like whipped cream?

JEROD H.
DAYTON, OH

Do you know if this store has X-rated videos?

(at a video store)

Paul D.
Los Angeles, CA

Guess what? I've just discovered the Eighth Wonder of the World. You!

Jarryd Z.
Toledo, OH

The world is coming to an end.
Have dinner with me.

Cassidy D.
Santa Barbara, CA

(STICK YOUR FINGERS IN A GLASS OF WATER AND FLICK SOME WATER ON YOUR INTENDED TARGET.)

Let's go to my place and get out of these wet clothes.

DENNIS W.
CHARLOTTE, NC

Wow!

ANONYMOUS

Am I that obvious? I feel like it's written all over my face.

(ACTUALLY WRITE PHRASES ON YOUR FOREHEAD, E.G., "TAKE ME," "YOU'RE HOT" OR "I WANT YOU.")

WADE M.
ORLANDO, FL

STUDS, STUDETTES, PLAYERS, AND MACDADDYZ!

We're looking for more of the BEST and WORST pick-up lines that have either gotten you in the door or your butt knocked to the floor. If it's original, and it works for any of us, we'll put it in the next book along with your name and hometown. Please include your name and address in case we want to get a hold of you.

Write to us at:

buzz boxx
P.O. Box 40671
Indianapolis, IN 46240-0671

E-mail us at:

buzzboxx@aol.com

Legal junk. Of course if you do submit a line, you're willingly sending it to us, you're over 18 years old, you're releasing all rights to it, you're giving us permission to use it any way we want . . . blah, blah, blah. (Our lawyer made us add this stuff . . . are you happy, Dave?)

Hey you! This is our blatant attempt to sell more books!

Did you know buzz boxx has other books besides this one? Look for these buzz boxx titles at cooler stores that "get it" (as in understand the *slacker* set):

1. *The Little Black Book of Dating Ideas*